DIFFERENT FAMILIES

By Steffi Cavell-Clarke

CRABTREE
PUBLISHING COMPANY
WWW.CRABTREEBOOKS.COM

Published in Canada
Crabtree Publishing
616 Welland Avenue
St. Catharines, ON
L2M 5V6

Published in the United States
Crabtree Publishing
PMB 59051
350 Fifth Ave, 59th Floor
New York, NY 10118

Published by Crabtree Publishing Company in 2019

©2018 BookLife Publishing

Author: Steffi Cavell-Clarke

Editors: Kirsty Holmes, Janine Deschenes

Design: Jasmine Pointer

Proofreader: Melissa Boyce

Production coordinator and prepress technician (interior): Margaret Amy Salter

Prepress technician (covers): Ken Wright

Print coordinator: Katherine Berti

Photographs

All images from Shutterstock

Printed in the U.S.A./122018/CG20181005

Library and Archives Canada Cataloguing in Publication

Cavell-Clarke, Steffi, author
    Different families / Steffi Cavell-Clarke.

(Our values)
Includes index.
Issued also in print and electronic formats.
ISBN 978-0-7787-5425-1 (hardcover).--
ISBN 978-0-7787-5448-0 (softcover).--
ISBN 978-1-4271-2220-9 (HTML)

    1. Families--Juvenile literature. I. Title.

HQ744.C38 2018   j306.85   C2018-905489-1
                                          C2018-905490-5

Library of Congress Cataloging-in-Publication Data

Names: Cavell-Clarke, Steffi, author.
Title: Different families / Steffi Cavell-Clarke.
Description: New York : Crabtree Publishing Company, [2018] |
  Series: Our values | Includes index.
Identifiers: LCCN 2018043786 (print) | LCCN 2018045318 (ebook) |
  ISBN 9781427122209 (Electronic) |
  ISBN 9780778754251 (hardcover) |
  ISBN 9780778754480 (pbk.)
Subjects: LCSH: Families--Juvenile literature.
Classification: LCC HQ744 (ebook) | LCC HQ744 .C38 2018 (print) |
  DDC 306.85--dc23
LC record available at https://lccn.loc.gov/2018043786

CONTENTS

Words that look like **this** can be found in the glossary on page 24.

WHAT ARE VALUES?

Values are the ideas and beliefs that we feel are important. They might include showing family members **respect** or keeping our communities clean. Sharing values with others helps us work together in a **community**. Values teach us how to respect each other and ourselves.

Sharing your ideas

Listening to others

Understanding different beliefs

Values make our communities better places to live. Think about the values in your community. What is important to you and the people around you?

Making safe choices

Being responsible

Respecting others

WHAT IS A FAMILY?

A family is a group of people who care about each other, and are usually **related**, either by birth, by marriage, or by **law**. Often, families live together in one household. There are different kinds of families around the world.

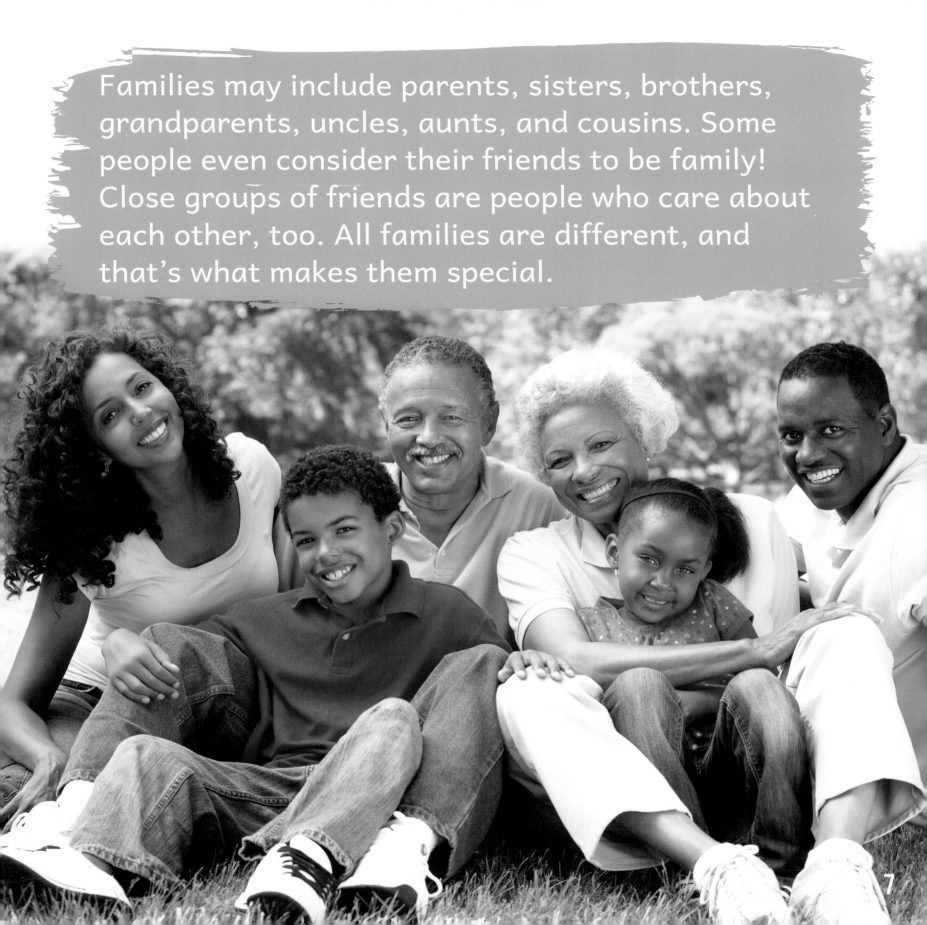

Families may include parents, sisters, brothers, grandparents, uncles, aunts, and cousins. Some people even consider their friends to be family! Close groups of friends are people who care about each other, too. All families are different, and that's what makes them special.

WE NEED FAMILY

We all have people in our lives that take care of us and make us feel special. For many, these people are their family. People depend on their families for support and love. Children depend on their families to help and **protect** them.

Families often do things together, such as celebrate special events.

The members of our families can teach us about our values. They can help us understand what is right and wrong, and also help us decide what we believe. It is important to have healthy **relationships** with our families. This means we treat each other with respect.

DIFFERENT FAMILIES

Some family members look like each other, and some do not.

How families are made up can differ widely. Some families have one child, two children, or more. Some have twins and some have triplets. Other families don't have any children at all.

Families can have one parent or two. Families with two parents can have a mother and father, two mothers, or two fathers. Every family is unique!

Many children live at home with their parents who look after them. Some children spend some time living with one parent, and some with another. Some children live with parents and grandparents. Families do not always have to live together in one home, all the time.

Oliver and his family eat dinner together every evening at their home. They enjoy their food and talk about their day. Oliver likes to tell his family all about school and his friends.

Sharing thoughts and feelings with family members is a good way to build healthy family relationships.

13

SAME-SEX PARENTS

Having same-sex parents means that your parents are both **female** or both **male**. Having same-sex parents is normal! Two men or two women can have a healthy relationship, choose to get married, and care for children just as any other couple can.

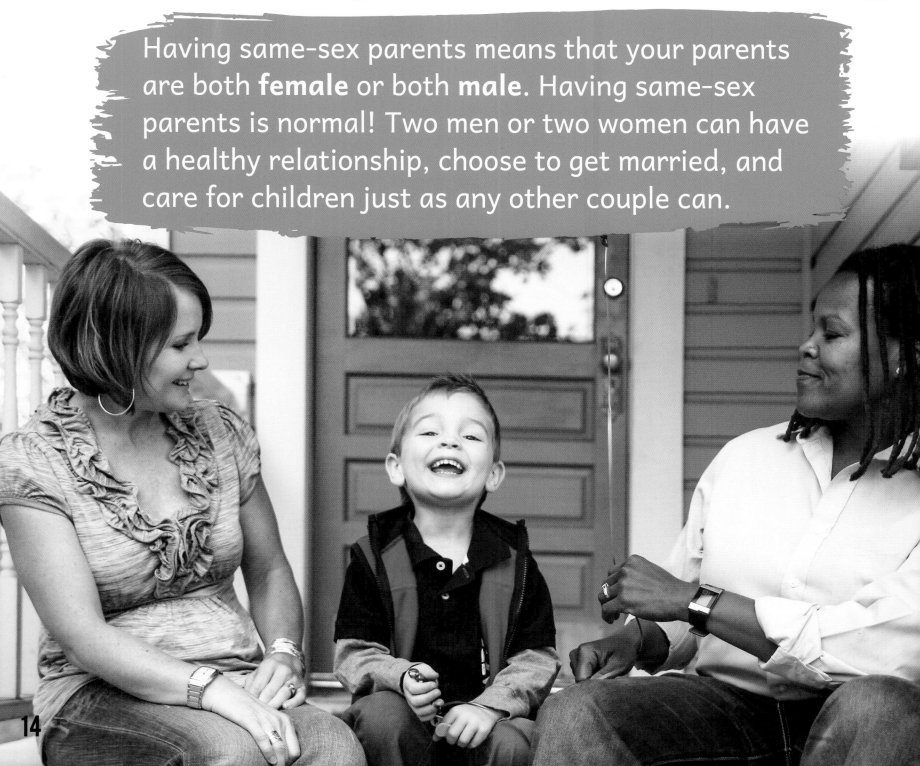

Rosie lives with her two fathers. She uses the name "Papa" for one of her fathers, and "Dad" for the other. They do many things as a family and make Rosie feel loved and cared for every day. They love to go for long bike rides as a family.

STEPFAMILIES

A stepparent is a parent who is married to the father or mother of a child. They join the family through this marriage. You do not have to be related to someone by birth to be part of the same family. Sometimes stepparents have children of their own who join the family by marriage too, and become stepchildren or stepsiblings.

Amy has two stepsisters. Her mother married the father of her stepsiblings. Now, they all live together at home. Amy doesn't look like her stepsisters, but they are still part of the same family. Their favorite thing to do is read books together.

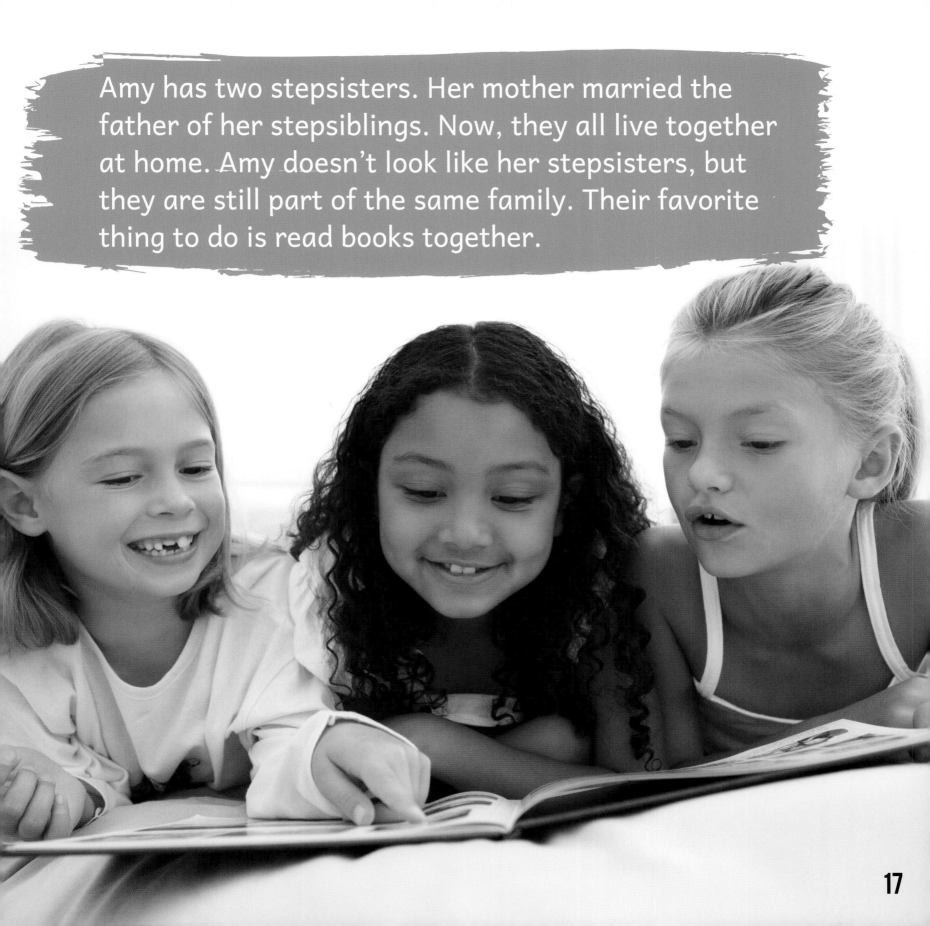

FOSTER FAMILIES

Sometimes, children cannot live with their parents or family members. This is usually because their parents are unable to care for them and provide them with the support they need. When this happens, children sometimes live with a **foster family** for some time.

Sometimes, children whose parents cannot care for them long-term are adopted by their foster parents.

Foster families help to raise children with love and care. Children can spend a few days or weeks with a foster family, or sometimes much longer. Some children may miss their parents or home when they are living with a foster family, but it is important that every child has a safe, secure, loving, and caring place to live.

ADOPTIVE FAMILIES

Families form in different ways. Many children are adopted into their families. When a child is adopted, their parents have chosen to bring them into their family. They did not join their families by birth.

Families do not need to be made up of people who are all related by birth. Families are made up of people who love and **value** each other. Every member of a family is equal and important.

21

FAMILIES SUPPORT US

In a family, you can share your feelings—the good ones and the bad ones—and know that your family will support you and help you. Families look after each other. Sometimes we experience emotions such as anger and frustration, and argue with other members of our family. However, it is important that we make up and forgive each other.

Being in a family means supporting each other and working together as a team. If you feel that you are having troubles with your family and cannot speak with them about it, then you should speak to an adult that you trust, such as a teacher. They will be able to help you.

GLOSSARY

community [kuh-MYOO-ni-tee] A group of people who live, work, and play in a place
female [FEE-meyl] Woman or girl
foster family [FAW-ster fam uh-lee] A family that officially takes in a child to care for them for a certain time period
law [law] Rule made by government that people must follow
male [meyl] Man or boy
protect [pruh-tekt] Look after or keep safe
related [ri-LEY-ted] Members of the same family
relationships [ri-LEY-shuhn-ships] Connections between people
respect [ri-SPEKT] Give someone or something the care or attention it deserves
responsible [ri-SPON-suh-buhl] Reliable or dependable
value [VAL-yoo] Treat something with importance

INDEX